HOLIDAYS

THANKSGIVING DAY

Let's Meet
THE WAMPANOAGS
and
THE PILGRIMS

by Barbara deRubertis
Illustrated by Thomas Sperling

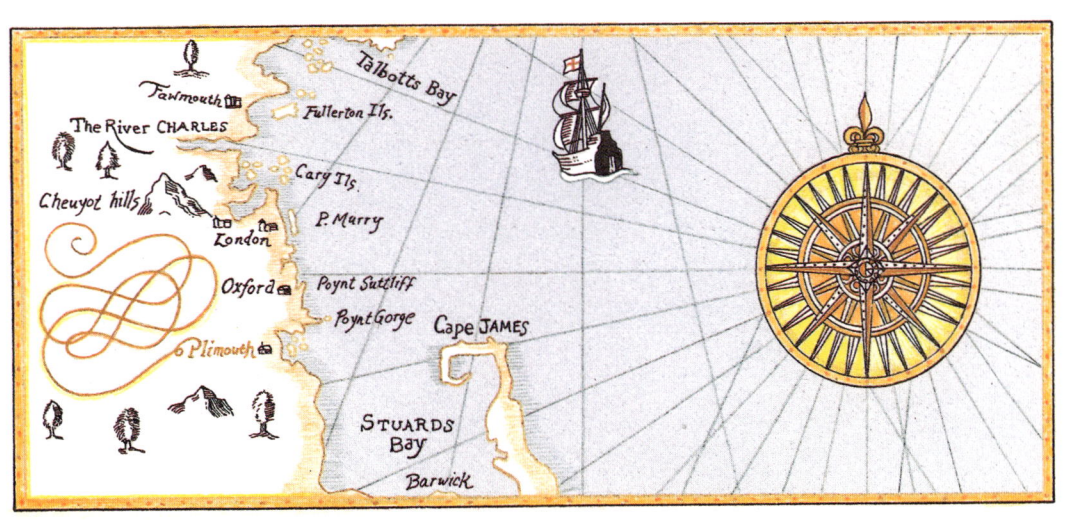

A map of the Massachusetts coast made by the explorer John Smith in 1614. All of these places were named by the King of England, James I.

The Kane Press
New York

Pronunciation Guide

Massasoit = MASS-uh-soyt
Wampanoag = WOM-puh-no-ug
Sachem = SAH-chum
Massachusetts = MAS-uh-CHOO-sits
Plimouth (old spelling) ⎫
⎬ PLI-muth
Plymouth ⎭
Patuxet = Puh-TUX-ut
Samoset = Sam-oh-set
Squanto = SKWAN-toe

Copyright © 1992 by The Kane Press
All rights reserved. No part of this book may be reproduced or transmitted in any form or by any means, electronic or mechanical, including photocopying, recording, or by any information storage and retrieval system, without permission in writing from the publisher. First published in the United States of America in 1992 by The Kane Press. Printed in the United States of America.

ISBN 0-7915-1911-2

10 9 8 7 6 5 4 3 2 1

Massasoit was Chief of the Wampanoag. Each Wampanoag village had a leader called a "sachem." But Massasoit was Chief Sachem of *all* the villages. He was a wise and powerful leader.

Massasoit must have been worried when he heard that about one hundred English settlers had come to his land!

It was November 11, 1620 when these settlers first arrived on a ship called the *Mayflower*. The ship dropped anchor off the coast of land now part of the State of Massachusetts.

Some of the people on board ship were called "Pilgrims." They had come to this land to find freedom. Others who traveled with them were also hoping to find a better life.

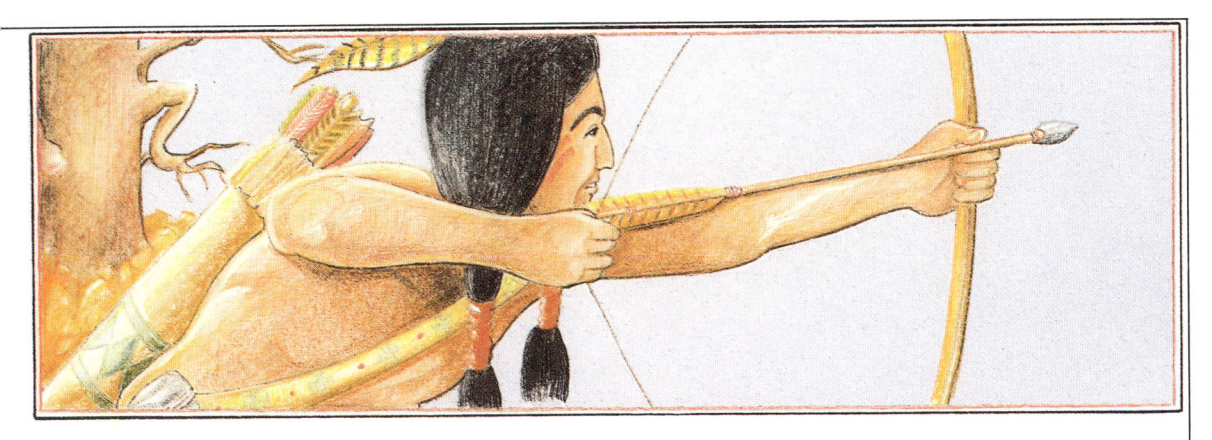

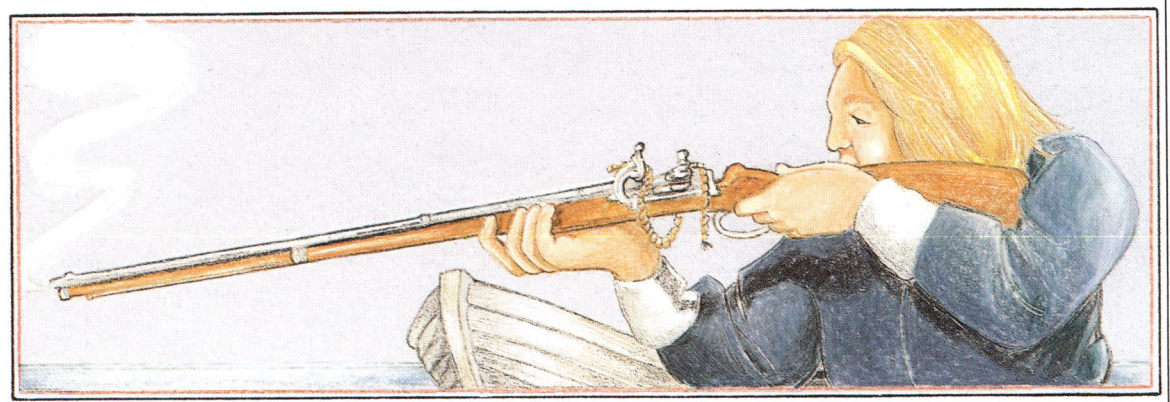

For weeks the Pilgrims looked for a good place to settle. One time, arrows were shot at them. They fired back with their muskets.

No one was hurt. But everyone was worried. The Wampanoags were worried about these English settlers. The English were worried about the people they called "Indians."

Finally, the Pilgrims found a good harbor at the place named Plimouth on their map.

After November came **December**.
Then the season of WINTER began.

*Winter at Plymouth was black and white.
It was dark and damp and cold.
The grey of hunger and sickness arrived,
and tales of sadness were told.*

At Plymouth, the Pilgrims found land that had already been cleared. They did not know that the land had once been a Wampanoag village called Patuxet.

The settlers continued to live on the *Mayflower* while they built a Common House. It would be used as a storehouse and as a church.

After December came **January** and **February**.

The Indians must have wondered how the settlers could possibly survive the winter. They had arrived too late to plant crops. They did not have time to build warm houses.

In the coldest days of winter, the settlers almost ran out of food. Most of them suffered from terrible sickness. Only six or seven people remained healthy. They were kept busy taking care of all the others.

The Common House was used as a hospital.

Before the sickness was over, almost half of the settlers died.

Later, a Pilgrim named William Bradford wrote about this time. He said that those who took care of the sick showed true love for their friends.

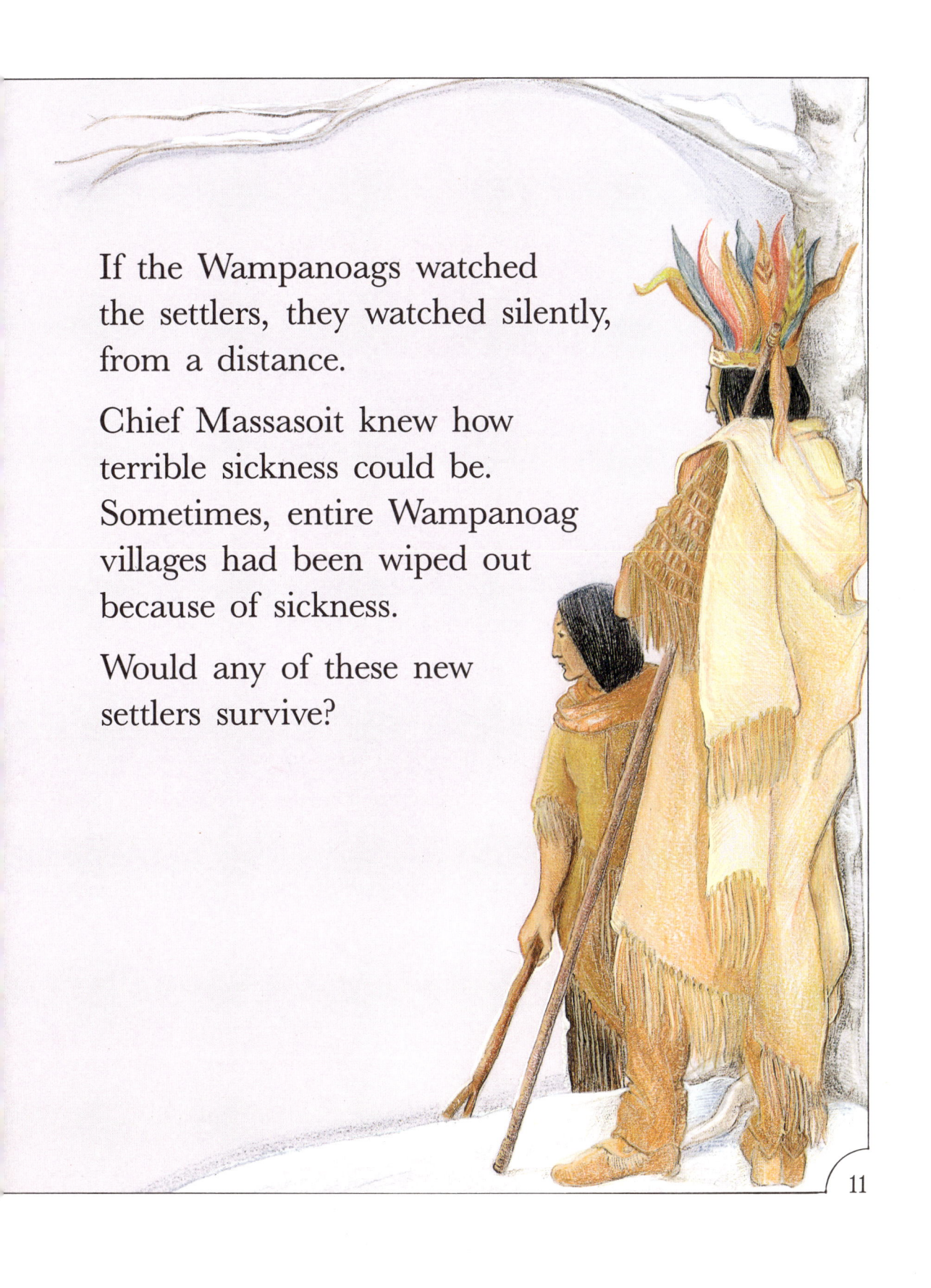

If the Wampanoags watched the settlers, they watched silently, from a distance.

Chief Massasoit knew how terrible sickness could be. Sometimes, entire Wampanoag villages had been wiped out because of sickness.

Would any of these new settlers survive?

After February came **March**.
The season of SPRING began.

Spring was painted a soft, new green
for the pastel flowers earth sends.
The season of hope arrived at last.
It came in the shape of friends.

In March, the first Indian visitor walked into Plymouth. Samoset surprised the settlers by greeting them *in English!*

On his third visit, Samoset brought a Wampanoag friend named Squanto, who spoke even better English.

Many years before, Squanto had been captured and taken to England. There he had learned to speak English. When he finally returned home to Patuxet, he was told that all the people of his village had died from a terrible sickness.

Squanto now told the settlers that Chief Massasoit himself was coming to visit them.

The Chief Sachem of the Wampanoags came with sixty of his people!
He had decided to make peace.
The settlers were weak, but they had powerful weapons.
The settlers could help his people.
And he could help the settlers.

Massasoit looked splendid.
The mulberry red paint on his face
showed he was an important leader.
He wore a turkey feather in his hair.
Around his neck hung beads of white bone.
His coat, leggings, and moccasins were
made of animal skins.

With a ceremony fit for a king, the settlers welcomed Massasoit. He was presented with gifts of knives, jewelry, and food.

Then, he was led to an unfinished house. Quickly, a rug and cushions were laid on the floor.

Drums rolled. Trumpets sounded. Six men saluted with their muskets. The Pilgrim leader, Governor John Carver, entered.
He bowed to kiss Massasoit's hand. Massasoit then did the same.

Chief Massasoit and Governor Carver made a peace treaty that lasted more than fifty years!

A Pilgrim later wrote that Massasoit was truly a great chief. He ruled by reason, not force. He always told the truth. And his word could be trusted.

After March came **April** and **May**.

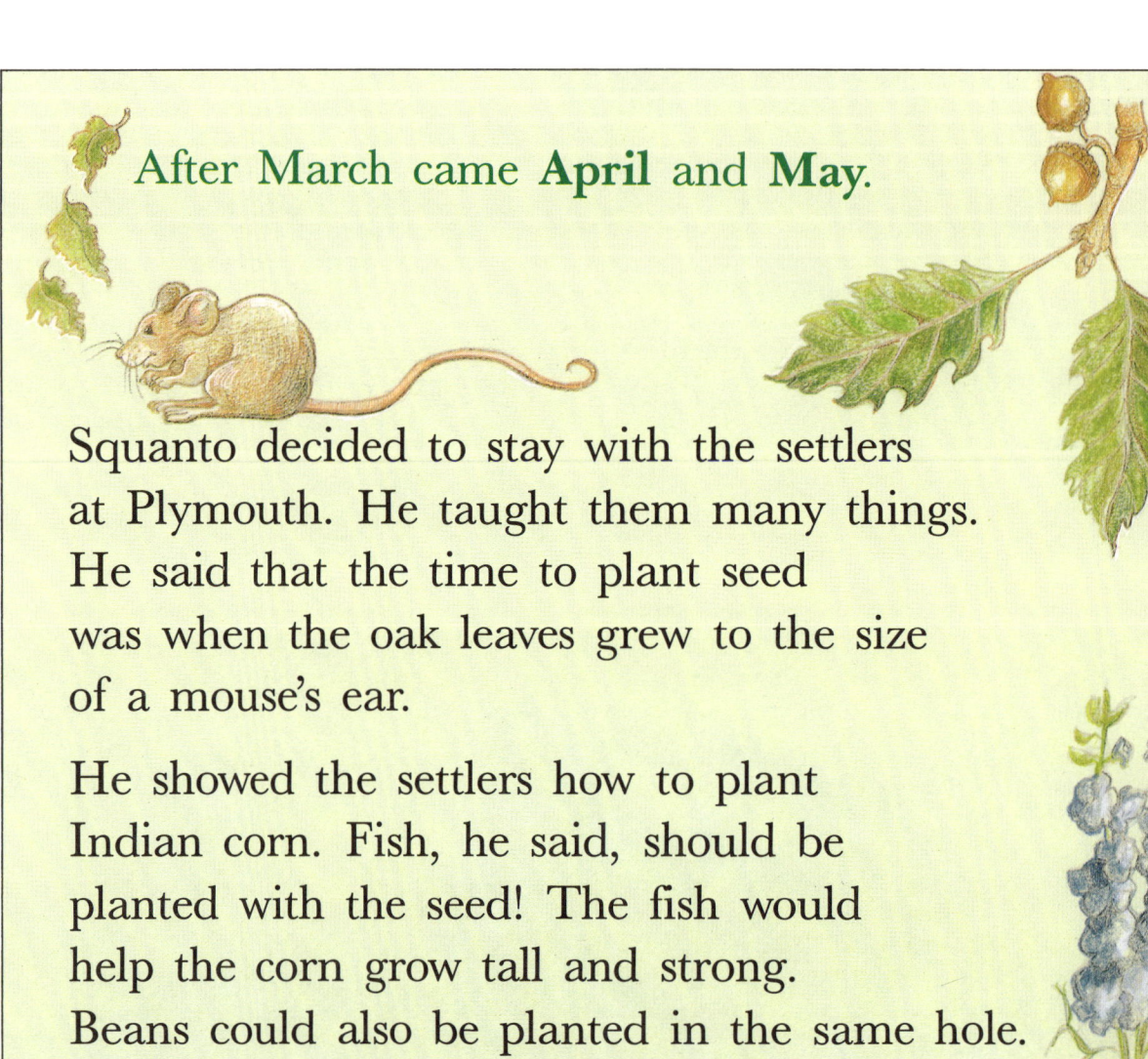

Squanto decided to stay with the settlers at Plymouth. He taught them many things. He said that the time to plant seed was when the oak leaves grew to the size of a mouse's ear.

He showed the settlers how to plant Indian corn. Fish, he said, should be planted with the seed! The fish would help the corn grow tall and strong. Beans could also be planted in the same hole. Their vines would climb up the corn stalks. And pumpkins could grow on the ground below.

During that Spring of peace and hope, a sad event happened. Governor Carver died. The settlers chose William Bradford as their new Governor.

The people of Plymouth must have thought he was a good governor. They elected him thirty more times!

William Bradford

After May came **June, July,** and **August**.
The season of SUMMER arrived.

*Summer brought Plymouth skies of blue
lit by a yellow sun.
The children picked bright red berries and plums
when the long day's work was done.*

Squanto also taught the settlers other things.
To catch fish.
To hunt deer with bow and arrow.
To dig clams and eels out of the mud.
To tap maple trees for sap to make syrup and sugar.
To know which plants were food, which were poison, and which were medicine.

The settlers worked in their fields. They finished seven houses built with pine boards and thatch roofs. They made beds, benches, stools, and tables. They dipped candles and made soap.

The children worked just as hard as their parents.

But on Sundays, the Pilgrims neither worked nor played. They went to church.

After August came **September** and **October**.
It was now the season of AUTUMN.

*Autumn was russet and golden and brown
like the ripened fields of corn.
The Indians and settlers were helping each other,
and Thanksgiving Day was born.*

Finally, the last of the harvest was brought in. The seed brought from England had done poorly. But the Indian corn harvest was excellent. The settlers would have plenty of food for the coming winter.

Governor Bradford decided it was a good time for a celebration. They would have a Thanksgiving festival at Plymouth!

Chief Massasoit, of course, must be invited. The settlers were very grateful to him and all the Wampanoag people.

Chief Massasoit certainly would have understood why the settlers wanted to have a Thanksgiving festival. The Wampanoags also had festivals to give thanks for a good harvest.

During their harvest festivals, the Wampanoags feasted, danced, held contests, and played games. They also gave part of what they had to the poor. And they gave something back to the earth.

They believed that people cannot just *take* without *giving*.

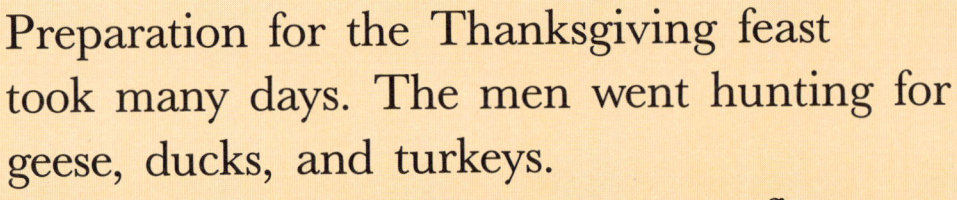

Preparation for the Thanksgiving feast took many days. The men went hunting for geese, ducks, and turkeys.
These would be roasted over open fires.

The four married women who had survived the winter did all the cooking.
It was a big job!
Of course, the children helped.

Corn was used to make bread and puddings.
Berries and plums made the puddings sweet.
Fish were simmered in steaming, thick soup.
Pumpkin was probably cooked over hot coals
or stewed—but not baked in pies.
The only pastries were made with meat.

Chief Massasoit arrived for Thanksgiving at Plymouth with ninety of his people! Fortunately, they also brought five deer as a gift. There were almost 150 people to feed.

Everyone enjoyed feasting on the delicious food. Then they put on shows for each other. The settlers marched and fired their weapons. The Indians showed their skills with bows and arrows.

They also held contests and played games. The Indians and Pilgrims were surprised to discover that many of their games were similar.

Everyone was having such a good time, the festival lasted for three days! Today, almost four hundred years later, we remember that festival when we celebrate Thanksgiving Day.

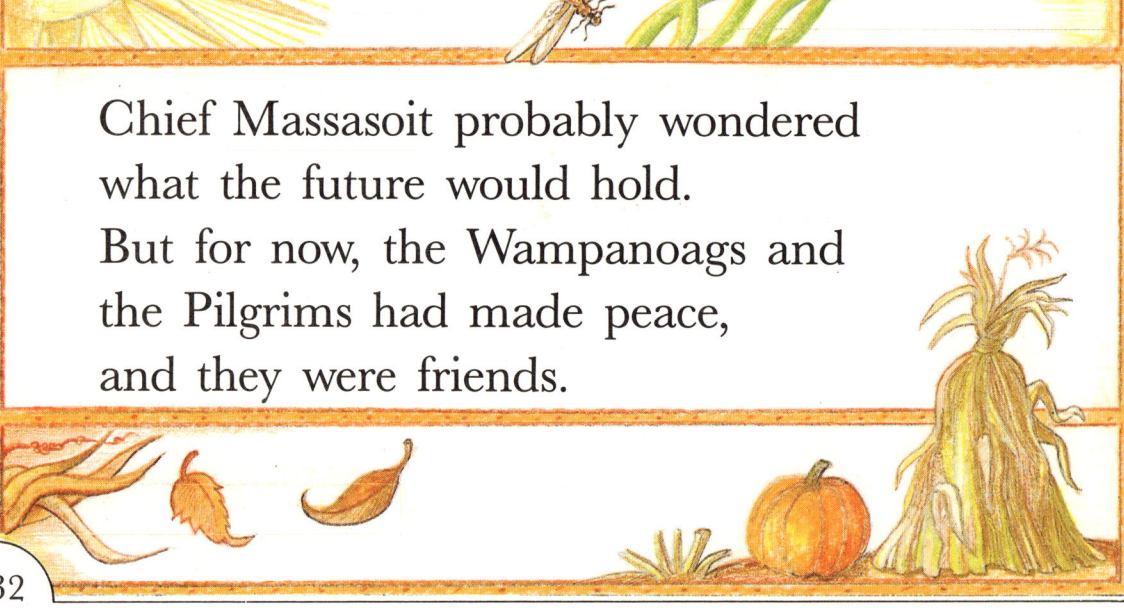

A year, with twelve months
and four seasons, had passed
for the settlers at Plymouth.

*The Indians and Pilgrims were different, it's true.
They were also much the same!
With talking and sharing, with helping and caring,
first peace, then friendship came.*

Chief Massasoit probably wondered
what the future would hold.
But for now, the Wampanoags and
the Pilgrims had made peace,
and they were friends.